Jack

The Healing Cat

By Marilyn Kallet

Illustrated by Sandra Van Winkle

Celtic Cat Publishing
Knoxville, Tennessee

For Samantha, Alaina, and yes, Jennifer!

HAPPY READING!

Marilyn + Jack

11/2017

In loving memory of Jack

Celtic Cat Publishing
2654 Wild Fern Lane
Knoxville, Tennessee
www.celticcatpublishing.com

Text Copyright © 2007 by Marilyn Kallet
Illustrations Copyright © 2007 by Sandra Van Winkle
Revised Edition (2010) by Celtic Cat Publishing
All Rights Reserved

Design by Sandra Van Winkle

ISBN: 978-0-9819238-5-7
Library of Congress Control Number: 2010908566

A story for children and adults about the healing power of pets. Jack, an abandoned kitten,
is rescued by a young girl, Heather. When Heather is sick, Jack becomes the catalyst for Heather's healing and he forms a new
relationship with Heather's father.

Mew!

I cried as loud as I
could from my little
cardboard box. I shivered so
hard my fur rippled.
Mew!
Did anyone hear me?

Sunlight
rushed in.
A little girl
leaned over me.
She gleamed
and smelled like
sunshine.

"Look, Mom!" she cried out!

"There's a kitty in this shoe box!"

She scratched my head with her fingertips.
Mommy, let's take him home!"

We'll have to see if he wants to stay
with us, Heather," her mother
replied.

Heather picked me up carefully.
She was not furry, but I liked her.
She held me and warmed me.
Friend!

But where were we going?

My tummy did not like
being moved around.

MEOW!

I stepped outside and **rolled** around to feel the silky grass all over me.

"I'm home!" I purred.

Heather set me down on a soft blanket in a big box.

Heather offered me a
bowl of milk.

It tasted velvety and
sweet on my tongue.

I lapped up the milk,
and licked my whiskers
clean.

"Heather, that cat can stay on the back porch, but he cannot come inside!" a man growled.

"I'm sorry, kitty!" Heather said. "My daddy never had a pet when he was growing up."

"Maybe he's afraid of you!"

Heather patted my head and told me,
"I will name you Jack,
like the boy in the song:

Are you sleeping, Brother Jack?"

Every morning she came out to feed me fresh kitty chow and to give me clean water.

I greeted her by rubbing against her and purring.

She laughed every time.

A happy way to start the day!

In the afternoon,
she dangled a toy mouse
that smelled so good it
made me dizzy!

I leaped,
batting at the
mouse with
my paw.

Each time someone opened the back
door, I dashed into the house.

I knew Heather lived there.

Why didn't I belong inside?

But Heather's daddy always caught me with his huge hands.

He picked me up and threw me out into the yard.

MEOW!

Good thing I have soft landing pads on my paws!

One day Heather did not come out to play.
Her mommy fed me, but she did not pet me.

I waited.

The house stayed too still.
I could not hear Heather's laughter or her singing.

She needed me!

When her mother opened the door, I slipped into the house.

My sharp ears picked up awful sounds of sobbing and coughing.

Poor Heather!

I raced to her room...

...and jumped up
on the bed!

I circled on her pillow and settled down next to her head.
I wanted her to
feel me
purring.

Then I rubbed my nose on
her cheek.

But she lay still.
She seemed very tired.

So I tried again..

I stood up and tickled her
cheek with my tail.

This time my
kitty magic worked.
She giggled!

When Heather's mother saw us, she said,
"Good boy! Heather is finally resting!"

Her dad agreed, "Heather's breathing sounds
better! That cat calmed her down!"

I did not leave
Heather that night.

Next morning, when she found me on the bed, she cheered, "Jack, you are such good medicine!"

Time for me to go outside.
Heather's dad lifted me gently,

and put
me down
on all fours
in the yard

Instead of kitty chow, he set out a bowl of tuna.

Heavenly!

"Heather's eating today for the
first time in days," he said.
"She likes tuna, too!"

After Heather got well, I slept
on her bed every night.

I snuggled by her side.

I grew fluffier.

Each day, when Heather came home from school, she dangled my ragged old mouse.

I danced on my hind legs!

I came and went as I pleased.
No one ever threw me out again.
Heather and I had chosen each other.

I was family, the grey fur brother, Jack.

Are you sleeping,
are you sleeping,
Brother Jack?

CPSIA information can be obtained
at www.ICGtesting.com
Printed in the USA
LVIC06n2226280916
506631LV00003B/5

* 9 7 8 0 9 8 1 9 2 3 8 5 7 *